How We Use

Wool

Chris Oxlade

Raintree
Chicago, Illinois

© 2004 Raintree
Published by Raintree, a division of Reed Elsevier, Inc.
Chicago, IL 60602
Customer Service 888-363-4266
Visit our website at www.raintreelibrary.com

For more information address the publisher:
Raintree, 100 N. LaSalle, Suite 1200, Chicago IL 60602

Printed and bound in China by South China
   Printing Company.

08 07 06 05 04
10 9 8 7 6 5 4 3 2 1

**Library of Congress Cataloging-in-Publication
Data:**
Oxlade, Chris.
  How we use wool / Chris Oxlade.
      p. cm. -- (Using materials)
Includes bibliographical references and index.
Contents: Wool and its properties -- Where is wool
from? -- Wool round the world -- Wool yarn -- Weaving
wool -- Knitting wool -- Wool colors -- Woollen clothes
-- More wool fabrics -- Wool carpets -- Making wool
better -- Sheepskin wool -- Wool and the environment.
  ISBN 1-4109-0599-3 (hc) 1-4109-0998-0 (pb)
 1. Wool--Juvenile literature. 2. Textile craft--Juvenile
literature.
[1. Wool.] I. Title. II. Series: Oxlade, Chris. Using
materials.
 TS1547.O93 2004
 677'.31--dc21

                                                    2003007433

Acknowledgments
The publishers would like to thank the following for
permission to reproduce photographs:
p.4 M. Kalab/Visuals Unlimited; p.5 Nancy
Sheehan/Photo Edit; p.6, 16 David Cavagnaro; p.7 Jack
Fields/Corbis; p.8 Australian Picture Library/Corbis; p.9
Chuck Eckert; p.10 Noonan Photography Inc.; pp. 11,
13 Jonah Calinawan; p.12 Barry Kunk/Stan/Grant
Heilman Photography; p.14 Peter Kubal; p.15 M.
Angelo/Corbis; p.17 Colin McPherson/SYGMA/Corbis;
pp.18, 28 Jill Birschbach/Heinemann Library; pp. 19,
20, 21 Jacqui Hurst/Corbis; p.22 Mike
French/Meonshore Studios Ltd.; p.23 Stone/Getty
Images; p.24 Art Directors/TRIP; p.25 Layne
Kennedy/Corbis; p.26 Earl & Nazima Kowall/Corbis;
p.27 Thom Lang/Corbis; p.29 Corbis.

Cover photographs reproduced with permission of
Heinemann Library (Greg Williams) (top) and Corbis
(Jacqui Hurst) (bottom).

Every effort has been made to contact copyright
holders of any material reproduced in this book. Any
omissions will be rectified in subsequent printings if
notice is given to the publishers.

Contents

Any words appearing in bold, **like this,** are explained in the Glossary.

Wool and Its Properties

All the things we use at home, school, and work are made from materials. Wool is a material. We use wool for many different jobs. Most wool is used to make **fabrics.** Woolen fabrics are made into things such as sweaters, jackets, gloves, and blankets. We also make carpets and rugs from wool.

This is what wool fibers look like through a **microscope.** They have a scaly surface.

This cardigan has been **knitted** out of wool.

Properties tell us what a material is like. Wool is made up of hairs that we call **fibers.** Some wool fibers are only about as long as your pinky. Others can be as long as your arm. They are thinner than the hair on your head. Wool fibers are soft, wavy, and a little bit stretchy. Most wool fibers are white, but some are brown and some are black.

Don't use it!
The different properties of materials make them useful for different jobs. These properties can also make them unsuitable for some jobs. For example, wool is not a strong material. So we do not use it to make ropes.

Where Does Wool Come From?

Wool is a **natural** material. Wool **fibers** are hairs, just like the hairs on your head. Most wool comes from sheep. A sheep's coat, called a **fleece,** is made of wool. It keeps the sheep warm in cold weather.

Sheep shearers cut the fleece with electric clippers. A quick shearer can shear a sheep in less than one minute.

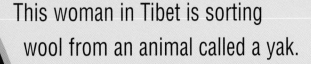

This woman in Tibet is sorting wool from an animal called a yak.

Once a year a sheep's fleece is cut off. This is called shearing. It does not hurt the sheep and the fleece soon grows back. The fleece is gathered together and sent to be processed. The wool is **greasy** and dirty, so it is cleaned first. Fibers from different areas of a sheep's body have different **properties.** Some fibers are short, thick, and rough. Others are long, fine, and soft. The fibers are sorted into different lengths depending on how they will be used.

Wool in the past

People have used wool as a material for thousands of years. At first they made clothes from the whole skins of sheep that they hunted for food. Then a few thousand years ago they discovered how to make wool into **fabrics** *by* **spinning** *and* **weaving.**

Wool Around the World

Most of the wool we use comes from sheep. Many different **breeds** of sheep live around the world. Each one has wool with slightly different **properties.** Some sheep have wool that feels very rough. Others have wool that feels very soft. The softest, finest wool comes from a breed of sheep called the merino.

These are merino sheep. They are bred for their soft wool.

8

Camel-hair fabric is fine and soft.

We use wool from other animals, too. Angora goats have very soft wool called mohair. Wool from cashmere goats makes very warm and comfortable clothes. Alpacas are animals like llamas that live in South America. Their wool is lightweight and warm. In Africa people make **fabrics** from wooly camel hair.

Don't use it!

It is important to choose the right sort of wool for a job. The wool must have the right properties. For example, cashmere wool is very soft and thin. The **fibers** *are weak. So we would not choose cashmere to make a carpet. It would wear out very quickly.*

Wool Yarn

Most wool is made into thread called **yarn.** A wool **fiber** is very thin and very weak. Wool yarn is much thicker and stronger than the fibers. Wool yarns are used to make woolen **fabrics.**

Looking through a **microscope,** you can see the fibers in yarn twisted together.

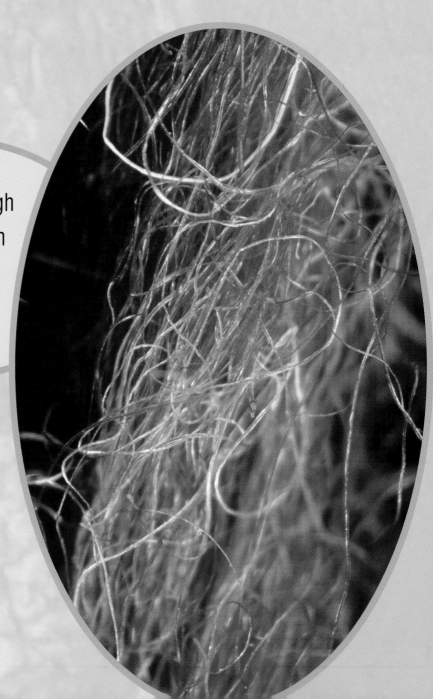

This close-up photograph shows part of a tapestry made with wool yarn.

Yarn is made by a process called **spinning.** The wool fibers are gathered together and then spun around so they twist tightly together. The fibers are **flexible** with rough scales so they cling together well. This is how long lengths of yarn are made from short fibers. Long, fine fibers are best for spinning. They make thin, smooth yarn called **worsted** yarn. Shorter, thicker fibers make thick, hairy yarns called woolen yarns. Different yarns are used for different jobs, such as making fabric and tapestries.

Weaving Wool

Most wool **yarn** is made into woolen **fabrics.** There are many different sorts of woolen fabric. Each one has different **properties.** For example, a fabric called tweed is thick with a hairy feel. It is made from woolen yarn. A fabric called gabardine is thin and smooth, and can be made from **worsted** yarn. Woolen fabrics stretch but go back into shape afterward. They are warm to wear.

This close-up photograph shows the yarns in woven fabric going over and under each other.

Weaving is one way of making yarns into woolen fabrics. To weave a fabric, lengths of yarn are passed over and under each other. Weaving is done on a **loom.** An automatic loom is a machine that weaves fabric very quickly. Some weavers make fabrics on a small hand-operated loom.

Woolen fabric is made on a machine called a loom.

Don't use it!
Most wool fabrics are not very strong. So wool is not a good material for making clothes that need to be tough, such as work overalls.

Knitting Wool

Wool **fabrics** are also made by **knitting.** Knitted fabrics have tight loops of **yarn** called stitches. The yarn in each loop goes through the loops next to it. This keeps the fabric together. Knitted woolen fabrics are thicker than **woven** fabrics. The loops of springy wool make them softer to touch. The loops also let the fabric stretch and go back into shape.

You can see the loops of yarn in this knitted fabric.

These patterns are made by knitting with special stitches.

Knitted fabrics can be made automatically on a knitting machine or by hand with knitting needles. Yarns for hand knitting are often very thick. They are made by twisting two or three other yarns together. They make thick, warm sweaters. Patterns can be made in fabrics by changing the size of the loops that are stitched and by using different sorts of stitches.

Knitting other fabrics

*Other yarns, such as cotton and polyester, can be knitted into fabric, too. These **fibers** are not springy like wool, and the yarns are tightly twisted. The fabrics are not as soft as knitted woolen fabrics.*

Wool Colors

Yarns and **fabrics** made of wool come in many bright colors and interesting patterns. When wool is sheared from a sheep it is white or light brown. People color the wool **fibers** with **chemicals** called **dyes.** Wool fibers are very good at taking in (or absorbing) the chemicals. We can dye wool fibers before they are **spun** into yarn, or we can dye yarn once it has been spun. We can also dye it after it has been made into a whole piece of fabric.

Woolen yarn can be colored by hand, using dye from **natural** materials like plants.

This woven fabric is called tartan. Colored yarns make the squared pattern.

Making patterns

Patterns in woolen fabrics are made by using different colors of yarn during **weaving** and **knitting.** In weaving, different colored yarns are used up and down the fabric and across the fabric. In knitting, different colored yarns are used for different loops or stitches.

Tapestry

Woolen yarn is used in a craft called tapestry. The yarn is threaded through holes in a piece of cloth to make tight loops. Patches of different colors of yarn make up patterns and pictures in the tapestry.

Woolen Clothes

The **properties** of woolen **fabrics** make them good for clothes. Some wool fabrics feel soft next to your skin, but others are rougher and can feel itchy. They are warm because air is trapped by the woolen **fibers,** which stops heat from moving through the fabric. This **insulates** your skin from the cold air. Woolen clothes are stretchy so they spring back into shape well. However, woolen fabrics must be cleaned carefully so that they do not shrink.

Woolen clothes shrink if they are washed in hot water.

In winter, we often wear woolen gloves to keep our hands warm, but they do not keep water out if they get covered with snow.

We use woolen fabrics for all sorts of clothes. Knitted woolen gloves, hats, scarves, socks, and sweaters are warm in winter. Pants and suits made from **worsted** fabrics are also very warm.

Don't use it!

*There are millions of tiny spaces between the fibers in woolen fabrics. If it is wet and windy they let water into the fabric. So we cannot use woolen fabrics on their own to make **waterproof** and **windproof** clothes.*

More Wool Fabrics

We use wool to make many other objects besides clothes. Woolen **fabrics** are good materials for covering furniture such as chairs and sofas. They are warm and soft to sit on, and they do not wear out quickly. They also stretch a little bit so they fit neatly over shapes like cushions. Blankets and rugs can also be made from wool.

Rugs such as these can be made out of wool.

Felt is a good material for making soft toys and models.

Felt

Felt is made by putting layers of wool **fibers** on top of each other and pressing them together with a steam iron. Sometimes glue is used to help the fibers cling to each other. Felt is a soft, weak fabric that is easy to pull apart. It soaks up liquids very well. It is also cheaper to make than **woven** or **knitted** fabrics. We can make table covers, hats, and slippers from felt.

Wool Carpets

Many carpets and rugs are made from wool. The woolen **yarn** is soft and warm, so it is comfortable to walk on. Wool carpets also help to keep homes warm. The yarn is not very tough, so wool carpets wear out if people walk on them in shoes. We can make wool carpets last longer by mixing the wool with tougher **fibers** such as **nylon.**

You can see the loops of wool in this close-up photograph of a carpet.

Carpets can be made by hand on looms such as this one.

Making carpets

Only the top part of a carpet is made of wool. It is called the pile. It is made up of loops of yarn. The loops are stitched to a strong fabric underneath called backing. Sometimes each loop is cut in half to make two ends that stick up. Some carpets have long pile. They feel very soft and warm. Most carpets are made on special carpet **looms.**

Don't use it!

Wool carpets in our homes can last a long time. Wool is not a good material for a carpet in a busy school, though. There, hundreds of people walk in shoes every day, which would wear away the wool.

Making Wool Better

Sometimes wool is not quite the right material for a job. We can still use wool by changing its **properties.** Wool **fibers** are often mixed with other sorts of fibers to make **yarns** and **fabrics.** The mixed fabric has the properties of both the fibers.

This is a pair of tights seen under a microscope. They are made from nylon and wool.

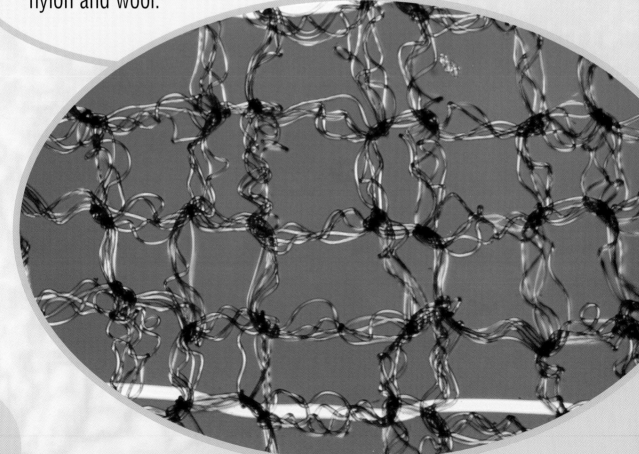

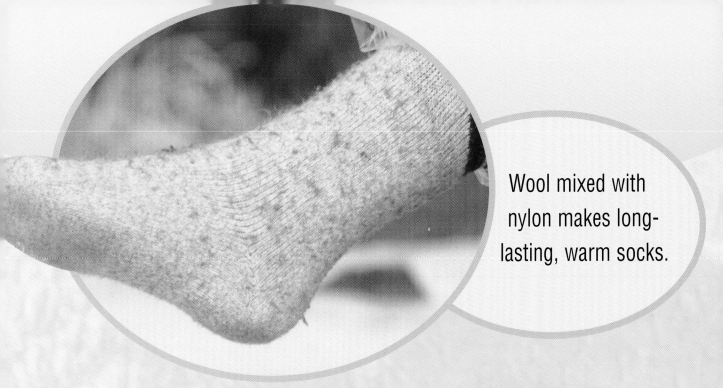

Wool mixed with nylon makes long-lasting, warm socks.

Many carpets have a mixture of wool and **nylon** fibers. Nylon is a strong **artificial** fiber made from **chemicals.** The wool makes the carpet soft and warm. The nylon makes the carpet last longer. Some socks have a mixture of wool and nylon, too. The nylon makes the socks last longer and stops them from shrinking when they are washed.

Finishing wool

Wool fabrics can be made better by treating them before they are used. This is called finishing. For example, a process called singeing makes fabric feel very smooth. It burns away the ends of fibers that stick out of the fabric. Singeing is used on fabrics for nice clothes, such as suits.

Sheepskin Wool

Sheepskin is leather with wool **fibers** on one side. Sheepskin is smooth on one side and wooly on the other side. It is **waterproof,** and is very warm. Sheepskin is made from the skins of sheep that are raised for their meat. The skin is treated with many different **chemicals** to turn it into leather. This process is called tanning.

A sheepskin hat keeps this man warm in cold weather.

Handcream often contains lanolin from sheep's wool.

Sheepskins can be made into cosy rugs and car seat covers. Sheepskins are also cut into shapes and stitched together to make warm clothes such as coats, hats, and boots. The wool is normally put on the inside of the clothes. This traps heat from the body, keeping the person warm.

Lanolin

*A sheep's wool is covered with **grease,** which is removed when the wool is cleaned. The grease contains a valuable oil called lanolin. Lanolin makes skin feel smooth and helps to keep it from getting dry, so it is used in creams and **cosmetics.***

Wool and the Environment

Wool is a **natural** material from animals. Wool will never run out because we can always keep raising sheep. We can throw wool away because it **rots** and does very little harm to the environment. However, the **chemicals** we use to clean and **dye** wool and to tan sheepskins can harm the environment. For example, these chemicals could harm fish if they leaked into a river.

You can recycle wool by putting old clothes in drop boxes or recycling bins.

Raising sheep for wool does not harm the evironment.

Recycling and reusing wool

We can use some wool again instead of throwing it away. This is called **recycling.** Old wool **fabrics** are pulled apart to get the **fibers** out. These are used to make new fabrics. Wool that has never been used is called new wool. Wool that has been recycled is called recovered wool or reused wool. You can reuse wool at home, too. For example, you can use old wool clothes as rags instead of buying new cleaning cloths.

Find Out for Yourself

The best way to find out more about wool is to investigate wool for yourself. Look around your home for wool and woolen things. Think about why wool was used for each job. What **properties** make it suitable? You will find the answers to many of your questions in this book. You can also look in other books and on the Internet.

Books to read

Ballard, Carol. *Science Answers: Grouping Materials: From Gold to Wool*. Chicago: Heinemann Library, 2003.

Hunter, Rebecca. *Discovering Science: Matter*. Chicago: Raintree, 2003.

Using the Internet

Try searching the Internet to find out about things having to do with wool. Websites can change, so if one of the links below no longer works, don't worry. Use a search engine, such as www.yahooligans.com or www.internet4kids.com. For example, you could try searching using the keywords "sheep," "loom," and "wool recycling."

Websites

www.bbc.co.uk/schools/revisewise/science/materials/

A great site that explains all about different materials.

www.wool.com/about/education.shtml

A useful site that explains where wool comes from and how it is used.

Glossary

artificial anything that is not natural

breed to raise animals for their fleece or their meat

chemical substance that we use to make other substances, or for jobs such as cleaning

cosmetic substance that people use to clean themselves or for makeup

dye colored chemical that soaks into a material to change its color

fabric flat sheet of bendable material, such as cotton or leather

fiber long, thin, bendy piece of material

fleece woolen coat of a sheep or the skin and wool together

flexible can be bent easily

greasy covered with oil

insulate to stop heat from escaping

loom machine used to weave fabric from yarn

knitted fabric made from yarn by making linked loops

microscope instrument used to look at things more closely. Microscopes make things look much larger.

natural describes anything that is not made by people

nylon artificial material, like plastic, that can be made into fibers

property quality of a material that tells us what it is like. Hard, soft, bendable, and strong are all properties.

recycle to use material from old objects to make new objects

rot to be broken down

spinning to twist together. Short fibers are spun together to make long yarn.

waterproof describes a material that does not let water pass through it

weaving making fabric by passing lengths of yarn over and under each other

windproof describes a material that does not let wind through

worsted fabric made from fine, long woolen fibers

yarn long, thin piece of material made by twisting fibers together

Index